21 Days of Prayer Impact

Kim Y. Lyons

<u>DEDICATION</u>

I dedicate this book to God, and I thank Him for the inspiration to join my faith with other believers to impact His Kingdom.

I also dedicate this book to our children and to my amazing husband; my encouraging, inspiring and loyal companion, whose strength, faith and constant love has made this journey with God the most incredible experience in my life!

I love you....

ACKNOWLEDGMENTS

I would like to thank Erica Davenport who volunteered to help make the Prayer Impact prayer line possible with her timeless efforts and morning dedication over the years.

I would also like to acknowledge gratefully writing consultant and publisher, Dr. Leah McCray for her invaluable help and push in preparing this book for publication. I appreciate you!

I am thankful for my Church Family at In Faith Ministries International and the people who have called into Prayer Impact every month from all over the world for your continual effort to pray and join your faith with mine to make a difference in this world.

INTRODUCTION

Life is so much easier when we pray and especially when we join our faith together...It can be simply amazing!

I love to pray and fellowship with the Lord, and as I was communing with God one day, He inspired me to initiate a prayer call line for people to call in and join their faith with mine to impact our lives and the lives around us.

The effectual fervent prayer of a righteous man availeth much. (James 5:16). So much more is accomplished when we join our faith together!

21 Days of Prayer Impact are corporate prayers that I've prayed over the years. I've chosen them with the intention of helping you focus your prayers to have an impact in your personal areas of concern and for others.

I believe as you pray these prayers by faith; the Holy Spirit will begin to move powerfully in your life.

Get ready for a move of God!

Table of Contents

DAY 1

If ye abide in me, and my words abide in you, ye shall ask what ye will, and it shall be done unto you. John 15:7

Remain in God, regardless of what it looks like. He is Faithful!

Lord, thank you for another day to be able to approach your throne of glory; for another day of protection through the night. Thank you for the blood of Jesus that has covered our homes as we have slept, and now we pray, Lord, that you will release your angels to fight for us in the heavenlies against principalities that would try and come against us. We pray that you would send your angels out to prosper our way in every area of our lives.

This morning we join our faith together, not for ourselves only, but for this country and the people of Israel. Lord, God, we pray that you would forgive us for our transgressions, and we humble our hearts before you Lord.

We pray for our President, for his family and for all the political leaders that are in position. We pray for every elected and appointed official that you have given to govern this country and our cities. We pray for our teachers and our leaders in the school system, and we pray that you would bring prayer back into the schools.

Lord, build up a spiritual wall of protection all around our leaders and give them wisdom and courage to hold up the constitution. Lord, we pray that you would begin to draw Christians into those appointed positions and that your presence would be evident in the lives of those who lead.

Lord, let your dominion be established in our country and among our leaders. Rule over our nations and allow us to be glad and rejoice that you are sovereign. Let the wicked be uprooted out of our land and save our nation.

We thank you for your grace and your mercy on this country, and we pray that you will continue to keep your hand of favor over this nation and that we do not take it for granted. Lord, bless us to exercise our right to pray for our country.

We thank you for releasing your favor into our lives, and we thank you that every step we take today will be the steps that you have ordered; for you have said that the steps of a good man are ordered by the Lord. Give us ears that we may hear what thus says the Lord. In Jesus name. Amen.

DAY 2

Let us therefore come boldly unto the throne of grace, that we may obtain mercy, and find grace to help in time of need. Hebrews 4:16

Eagerly approach his throne and find help. He cares for you.

Father, how sweet it is to have communion with you and we thank you for the relationship that we have in you. Thank you for waking us up to experience a day that we have never experienced before. We bless your name. Holy is the Lord, God, Almighty and we recognize your sovereignty.

We lift you up with all of our hearts, minds, and souls. We thank you, Lord, God, that even through your glory you have given us access to come boldly to your throne. What a privilege. Father, if you find anything in us that is not of you, we pray that you would remove it and forgive us for all of our sins and restore us to right relationship with you.

We thank you for life and life more abundantly. We thank you for the favor that has come upon our lives and our family. We thank you that we are in that set time of them of favor.

Lord, increase our finances. Lord, bless us today. Bless our storehouses. Bless us to be good stewards of the financial blessings that you've given to us. Lord, bless us to have more than enough to fulfill our destiny and assignment. Bless us not to lack any good thing as we delight ourselves in you. Bless us to be a blessing to others.

Give us a heart to give and a heart to understand that we need to honor you with the first of everything that you've given to us. Lord, bless us to learn how to give to you and to give to others first.

Give us a heart and compassion to think of others more highly than we think of ourselves. Bless our hands to be the ones that will bless others. Cause us to prosper in a supernatural way and send your angels now, in the name of Jesus, and begin to prosper our way.

Bless us with wisdom. Bless us not to be haughty and arrogant. Bless us to move in humility and to be a blessing to others. Bless us to live in such a way that you can trust us to give to the Kingdom and others. We pray that you would command a blessing over our lives and give us favor.

Lord, we bless your name today. We love you, and we thank you for open heavens. We bless your holy and righteous name. In Jesus name. Amen.

DAY 3

Then shall ye call upon me, and ye shall go and pray unto me, and I will hearken unto you. Jeremiah 29:12

He hears you!

Oh Lord, how precious and marvelous is your name. Thank you so much for waking us up and allowing us to have another day in your presence. We welcome your Holy Spirit, and we thank you for protecting us all through the night.

How excellent is your name, God. It is above all things, and we bless you for you are God and God alone. There is no one greater than you; as the deer pants for the water, so our soul's pant for you. We want more of you; to be like you and to walk in the authority that you have given us. Bless us to be effective in your Kingdom.

Father, we humble ourselves before you in the

name of Jesus. We plead the blood of Jesus which confirms our promise and power in you. We pray that you would stir up a passion and zeal to love you and to seek your word.

God bless us not to be so self-consumed that we forget about you. Lord, you are our first love. Father, we pray that you would stir up revival in us. Bless us to be excited about you and the Kingdom. Bless us to be on fire for you and to be bold and courageous.

Lord, burn up all the works of darkness that are working against our lives and the lives of our loved ones. We thank you that we have been redeemed from the curse of the law and that we have abundant life in you.

Lord, bless this mind that we have to be the same that is in Christ Jesus. Lord, bless us to act the way you act, to speak what you speak and to love how you love. God, bless us to seek your will and seek your face according to your word. Lord, bless us to study to show ourselves approved; a workman not ashamed, rightly dividing the word of truth.

Bless us to seek your face and to have quiet time

with you and to hear from you. Bless us to understand your word. Open the eyes of our understanding. Reveal to us the secret, hidden treasures of your word. Bless us to understand heavenly things, but, let us not to be so super spiritual that we are unrelatable and unable to minister to others.

Lord, open our eyes and let us behold the wondrous things out of your word. Bless us to walk in the confidence of your word. Bless us to stand on your word and not be moved. Reveal the things that belong to us. Let your glory be revealed in our lives. Bless it to be evident and obvious that we are the children of the most high God. Bless us to be good stewards over your glory and let us comprehend what is the breadth and depth and height of your love for us.

Lord, release dew from heaven into our lives. Bless us to walk and be used for greater works today. Guide us into your truth for your namesake.

Send your angels out right now in the name of Jesus. Those angels that you've given charge over our lives to bring provision. We thank you for the blessing and the revelation that is coming, and we thank you for the word that is growing on the inside of us.

We're excited about our call, excited about our purpose, excited that you have commanded a blessing on our lives so that we may be a blessing in your Kingdom. We love you, Lord, and we bless you today. In Jesus name. Amen.

DAY 4

Draw nigh to God, and he will draw nigh to you. Cleanse your hands, ye sinners; and purify your hearts, ye double minded. James 4:8

Arrest every thought that would try to prevent you from being focused on the Lord. Now confess your sins and enter into His Presence.

Father, you are holy, and we bless your name. You are beyond amazing, and we bless your name today for you are great; King of kings and Lord of lords.

Lord, we thank you for another opportunity to embrace a new day. We thank you for divine protection and for the angels that you have given charge over our lives. We thank you for your grace and mercy, and we understand that it is a privilege and a blessing to be among the living. Bless us not to take that for granted. We thank you for being a good God and for being faithful in and through our lives.

Lord, as we enter into your presence we come with

humility and thankfulness. Thankful for the opportunity to come boldly to your throne by the blood of Jesus, and we consider it a privilege to be able to release our petitions and prayers at your feet.

Lord, we enter in the name of Jesus, asking for forgiveness of sin. Remove those bad attitudes and hidden motives. Remove anything that can separate us from your glory. Purify us with your glory and make us righteous in your sight.

We thank you that we are the called in Christ Jesus. We thank you that we are redeemed through His blood that was shed on the cross. We thank you for allowing us to be joint heirs with Abraham of the covenant promise of blessing. Oh, God, we thank you that we have obtained an inheritance. Thank you for the victory that we have in Christ Jesus and that we are seated in heavenly places, even right now.

Let your kingdom come and your will be done, on earth, as it is in heaven. Let the gates of our lives be open for the King of Glory to come in and have access in every area. Lord, we bless you today in the name of Jesus, and we ask that you will bless our faith to grow exceedingly. Maximize your glory and your word in us, Father. In Jesus name. Amen.

DAY 5

But without faith it is impossible to please him: for he that cometh to God must believe that he is, and that he is a rewarder of them that diligently seek him. Hebrews 11:6

Your faith pleases God.

Father, we thank you so much that we have the boldness and the confidence to approach your throne and glory because of the blood of Jesus. We thank you for the blood that covers all of our sins, and that cleanses us from all unrighteousness.

Lord, we thank you for another day in your presence; one that we've never witnessed before and we enter into your presence with thanksgiving and praise. We bless your name and thank you for all the spectacular things that you've done in our lives. You are worthy to be praised. The angels bow before you and all heaven and earth adore you; what a mighty God we serve.

We magnify you and boast of you as you enlarge your presence in our hearts. Your throne is established forever, and we honor you.

Cleanse us from all unrighteousness and wash us clean with the blood of Jesus. Forgive our iniquity and burn off any works of darkness in our lives.

Thank you, Lord, for another day of divine protection and for protecting this country. We thank you for divinely connecting our hearts together so that we may corporately lift up your name.

Oh, God, bless our families with favor. Bless our destinies and propel us into the call that you have ordained for us. We will continue to speak of your glory and your goodness for the rest of our lives.

Let the confidence and schemes of the enemy be rooted out of our lives. Lord, baptize us with the fire of your Holy Ghost and stir up revival in our souls and our minds. God, continue to allow us to thirst and hunger after righteousness, only to be satisfied with your favor and blessing.

Put to shame those who wish evil on us, Lord. We thank you for our salvation and the salvation of our family members and friends. We are in expectation, Lord, and we thank you for delivering us from those spirits that try to attach themselves to us. We thank you for the liberating power of breakthrough. We thank you for all that you have done in our lives.

Now give us supernatural wisdom and revelation and open the eyes of our understanding so that we may know you. Give us a hunger and a thirst to seek your face.

Lord, bless us to prophesy, to teach the truth and to speak your word with power. We love you; we thank you, and we bless you. In Jesus name. Amen

DAY 6

And this is the confidence that we have in him, that, if we ask any thing according to his will, he heareth us: And if we know that he hear us, whatsoever we ask, we know that we have the petitions that we desired of him. I John 5:14-15

Ask!

Father, create in us a clean heart and renew a right spirit within us so that we will not sin against you. Please forgive us for all of our iniquities and wash us clean, making us as a body of believers who are righteous in your sight.

Lord, we are grateful for another day in your presence. We are grateful for another opportunity to join our faith together, in oneness and agreement, for your divine purpose. Thank you for watching over this country and our families. You are awesome, and we thank you for loving us so much.

We honor you. We salute you, and we lift you up as high as we can in our mind, soul, and heart. We adore you, and we thank you for protecting us through the night and for protecting our children. We thank you for all that you have done for us, Father.

We pray that you would bless the integrity and decisions of our President and all those who are in leadership positions in the governance of this country. We pray for our state, city and community leaders, in the name of Jesus. Give them supernatural wisdom as they make decisions that affect our lives and the lives of our children.

Oh, Father, we thank you that you have given us life in abundance. We are thankful that you looked down and decided to release blessing and favor on our lives and our families. We do not take that for granted. We appreciate you, Lord, and we are thankful for all that you have done.

Father, we ask for wisdom; the wisdom that you said you would release liberally. We ask that you lead and guide us in our conversations with our spouses, with people in our churches and with everyone that we encounter. Inspire us to give right counsel and do those things that are pleasing unto you and that meets the needs of your people so that they will grow and be edified in the spirit of love. We want to be more like you. We want to walk in your integrity and your wisdom.

God bless us not to procrastinate. Bless us to retrieve those things that we have put on the shelf; those things that you have inspired us to do and bless us to get them done. Bless us to be obedient to your word at the time that it is spoken in our hearts. It is our soul's desires that we will glorify you in every aspect of our lives. In Jesus name. Amen.

DAY 7

One thing have I desired of the Lord, that will I seek after; that I may dwell in the house of the Lord all the days of my life, to behold the beauty of the Lord, and to enquire in his temple. Psalm 27:4

Desire God fully with all of your heart, soul & mind.

Lord, we thank you for this incredible access that you've given us through the blood of Jesus. We can come boldly to your throne of glory and lay out our petitions, praise, and worship before you. We bless your name, and we glorify you.

We thank you for your wings of glory that has protected us during the night, and we thank you for hiding us in that secret place where no evil can come against your children. Thank you for your presence of glory that surrounds our homes and hearts this day.

How majestic is your name, oh, God. We love you and thank you for your grace and your mercy, ever being our deliverer and our redeemer. Thank you for life. We didn't even know that we were walking in darkness before you came into our life and we thank you so much.

Shake the heavens and fill our homes and our churches with your glory. Write upon the heavens and release your voice and your glory in the atmosphere of your presence. Cover us with your glory and consume us from the inside out. We want a spectacular encounter with you. Take us to another level of intimacy with you.

We pray and thank you for your hedge of protection around our minds and our children. We thank you for your protection around our bodies and our finances. Thank you for covering this country and the country of Israel. Thank you for your favor over our lives. Teach us wisdom and your ways. Lead us on the right path.

You are our source of wisdom, Lord. Give us an

understanding that we may minister properly to all those that you send into our lives. Remove the spirit of pride and jealousy. Let our lives be fruitful.

Release your rivers of blessing over our lives. Thank you so much that we have tasted and seen that you are good. Satisfy our mouth with good things today and bless us to release good things, encouraging words out of our mouths.

We give you glory today, and we love you, Lord. Keep the glory of revival flowing in our souls and minds. Thank you for all that you have done. We love you, and we magnify you, and we consider it all done. In Jesus name. Amen

DAY 8

Who shall ascend into the hill of the Lord? Or who shall stand in his holy place? He that hath clean hands, and a pure heart; who hath not lifted up his soul unto vanity, nor sworn deceitfully. Psalm 24:3-4

Examine your Heart.

Lord, we thank you for another day that we've never witnessed before, and we thank you for your presence in our lives. Thank you for keeping us covered and protected.

We ask that you would cleanse us from all unrighteousness and that you wash us clean with the blood of Jesus. Remove any sin that is in our hearts. Burn off any works of darkness that exist in us right now, in the name of Jesus. We pray for those who have ought against us and anyone whom we have harmed, knowingly or unknowingly, and we pray for forgiveness over them, and we ask for forgiveness.

Now we enter into your presence with the

confidence of knowing that we can ask anything in your name, and it shall be done.

We thank you that we have boldness in your presence by the blood of Jesus. We thank you for the blood of Jesus that gives us a covenant right of promise and relationship with you. Thank you for the authority that we have in you to bind every principality and every power that operates against our lives. We take authority over anything that will try and operate against this prayer in the name of Jesus. No weapon formed against us will prosper.

This is our set time for favor. This is our set time for miracles. We thank you that we have the victory in Christ Jesus. We thank you right now that no one has a strong arm or authority like you. You have created all things for yourself, and we praise you for your awesome power. Let the power of your hand be released in our lives.

Father, we know that you are a Father of miracles, and we pray for miracles today. You are a miracle worker. You have raised the dead, healed the blind and freed the bound. So we pray, in the name of Jesus, for miracles in our lives and the lives of our family members; miracles for deliverance, salvation, breakthrough, and healing. We pray for things that appear impossible because we know that all things are possible with you.

God, we cover all these petitions that are backed by the blood covenant that comes through your son, Jesus. We consider it done, and we glorify you. In Jesus name. Amen.

DAY 9

Surely goodness and mercy shall follow me all the days of my life: and I will dwell in the house of the Lord forever. Psalm 23:6

Remember goodness is following you, God is Faithful.

Lord, we thank you for the blood that gives us access. We thank you that we can enter into your Holiness with our petitions and our praise. We thank you for being such an incredible God.

If you find anything within us that is not of you, we ask that you cleanse us and forgive us for any unrighteousness. Lord, send your word and deliver us from any distractions. We choose to walk in the straight gate, and we thank you for all that you have given to us through the blood of Jesus. We claim the power and authority that activates in your name, and we break up any demonic covenant made by our ancestors, in the name of Jesus.

We pray for healing, and we confess that by your stripes we are healed. We stand on your word by faith, and we activate your power to heal our bodies, our minds, our spirit and our souls. We bind every spirit of infirmity that has come upon our lives and the lives of our family. We declare that they are healed in the name of Jesus.

Lord, we pray for restoration, revival and renewal in the lives of your people. Lord, we declare that we shall live and not die and see your goodness. We decree that no enemy will take our inheritance, and we will put no other gods before you. We pray that our hearts and our adoration will be toward you.

Father, remove those familiar spirits out of our lives that bring oppression and depression, and we decree and declare that it is done right now in the name of Jesus. We shall walk in your liberty and your Spirit. We shall do everything that you have said we will do. We shall have everything that you have said we will have. We are new creations, and our old nature has passed away. Behold you have made all things new.

Lord as we come to you, divide and scatter all

those that are joined against our lives and the lives of our children. We loose confusion by the blood of Jesus over every enemy and conspiracy against our lives, churches, families, and marriages. We declare victory in the name of Jesus; victory in the blood of Jesus.

Lord, we pray that you would guide us into all truth today. We thank you that we are made perfect in you through the blood of Jesus. That what you have begun in us you will complete. Let us not get weary in well-doing, for in due season we shall reap if we faint not. We thank you that no weapon formed against us shall prosper; that we are more than conquerors. Thank you that we have the power of your Holy Spirit activated on the inside of us.

Bless us to speak victory today. Bless us to declare that we have overcome. Father, God, we thank you that the manifestation of victory over the world is taking place right now. We believe for miracles to be released in the name of Jesus. We thank you that victory has been released through your Holy Spirit and we come in agreement that you will begin to do a great work in the Kingdom as you gather your people together.

Now send your angels out to lost souls, those whom we have prayed about and bring in the harvest right now in the name of Jesus. Send the laborers out, Lord, and give them words to say and a heart to manifest your love.

We pray that you will begin to do a stirring in the earth. Release your angels and your power for we know that the days are growing cold. We pray that your perfect will for humanity will be done. We proclaim your victory.

We thank you that we have the mind of Christ. Lord, bless us to walk in it today and to be bold and courageous. Bless us to be the light so that when people see us they will see your glory and know that we are children of the most high God. Bless us not to have a double lifestyle, to be one way around the Saints and act like the devil when we are by ourselves. Bless us to live this life of righteousness and obedience to your word.

We love you today, Lord. Command your blessings upon us and release ridiculous favor that will cause us to shout your praises. We love you, and we ask all these things, in Jesus name. Amen

DAY 10

Confess your faults one to another, and pray one for another, that ye may be healed. The effectual fervent prayer of a righteous man availeth much. James 5:16

Don't allow your sin to separate you from Gods presence.

Father, we thank you so much for your loving kindness, and we thank you for your grace and mercy. We thank you for a day that we have never seen before. We thank you for being our creator and holding all power in your hand. We love you with all of our heart, and we thank you for being our good shepherd over our souls.

This is the day that you have made, and we will rejoice and be glad in it. Father, we come now, in the name of Jesus, asking that you forgive us for all of our sins. Wash us clean with the blood of Jesus. Burn off every bit of darkness that is trying to grip our hearts.

We thank you for protecting us from unseen dangers, and we thank you for the angels that you've given charge over our lives. Lord, you are the best, and we love you. Lord, reveal yourself to men that they may know that you strive with us. Bless us to be so entangled in your spirit, with such oneness with you that we speak like you and love like you.

Bless us to be the ambassadors that you have called us to be; the children of light and the salt of the earth. Bless us to make a difference to those who are suffering and those who are lost. Let souls be saved because of our obedience to you and your love for humanity. Oh God, we pray that you would give us an obedient heart. Remove that rebellious spirit from us and give us an excellent spirit. Bless us to master good over evil. Bless us to love those that are unlovable and to be careful with our words so that we are not hurtful to others.

Strengthen us in our weak areas. Let those who seek to hurt us be clothed in shame. Thank you for this authority you have given us that whatever we bind on earth is bound in heaven and whatever we loose on earth is loosed in heaven. We bind principalities, powers, and rulers of darkness in high places, and we loose ourselves from the power of wickedness. We loose our finances from every spirit of poverty, debt, and lack. We loose our spirit from fear right now in the name of Jesus, and we walk in faith knowing that all things are possible through you.

Thank you for favor and victory. Bless this mind to be in us that was also in Christ Jesus. Father, we thank you that Christ rises up on the inside of us to take authority over every fleshly thought.

Release your angelic army to defend us. Release them to war against any spirit assigned to block our blessing. We pray that the flood gates of heaven will be open right now in the name of Jesus. Lord, release your strong-arm in our lives and scatter every enemy that tries to come up against us.

We love you Lord, God, and we thank you for every promise and every blessing. We thank you that your word is true in our lives. In Jesus name. Amen

DAY 11

Glory and honor are in his presence; strength and gladness are in his place. I Chronicles 16:27

Be quiet, be still & know that He is God.

Lord, we love you and you are worthy of all the praise. We exalt you, and we thank you for being so personal with each one of us. You are God; so great and yet so intimate on the inside of us. We thank you for that, and we exalt your name. We celebrate you, Lord. You are truly incredible, and we come boldly to the throne of grace, thanking you for the blood of Jesus that gives us access to enter into your presence.

We ask for forgiveness of all of our sins and iniquities. We pray that you wash us clean from the works of darkness that have entangled us and we pray that you would create a clean heart within us. We need your touch today. Anoint every moment of our day with your grace and goodness.

Bless us to be pleasing to you, Lord. We want to walk the walk that agrees with our confession that we are the children of God. We are your ambassadors and we want to effectively represent your Kingdom in the earth. This is the day that you have made and we delight in it. We thank you for your glory that woke us up this morning. We thank you for your faithfulness towards us and your loving kindness.

Teach us how to hold onto our faith without wavering. Teach us how to walk in integrity that is pleasing unto you. Thank you for being faithful to us and bless us to be faithful to you. Bless us not to be self-consumed. Remove the spirit of pride out of our lives. Bless us to walk in humility; to walk as Christ walked.

Holy Spirit rise up on the inside of us and take control of our hearts and our emotions. Guide us today and teach us, bring conviction and change. Bless us to guard our tongue and not be so quick to give our opinion. Bless us to be slow to take offense. Remind us that our mission and our assignment is to live this life for you and to be pleasing in your sight.

Bless our lives to be seasoned with prayer and compassion. Bless us to want to talk with you, not just when we need things, but to spend time with you and to have a passion to read your word and to show ourselves approved. Expand your love in our hearts.

Release your warring angels in the atmosphere to work on our behalf. Lord, heal our bodies and our minds. Heal marriages today for You are the great physician. You hold all power in your hand, and you can do all things. Our faith will not waver as we intercede for those that are going through sickness. We stand in agreement by faith that your healing anointing is released; right now, to touch all of those that we have been interceding for, in the name of Jesus. We are believing for miracles, signs, and wonders. Release your anointing and remove all deception and deceiving spirits out of out of our way in Jesus name.

Give us wisdom today Lord, God. We declare that no weapon formed against us will prosper. You are a God who is faithful. Bless us to go where you would have us to go. Bless us to rise up and be the righteousness of Christ. Bless us to be pleasing to you and let all the giants around us that are trying to destroy us fall now, in Jesus name.

Lord, have your way as we yield our will to your will. Let your perfect will be done on earth and in our lives so that you will get the glory. We will not glory in the flesh, but in you. We love you, and we give you all praise today. In Jesus name. Amen.

DAY 12

If my people, which are called by my name, shall humble themselves, and pray, and seek my face, and turn from their wicked ways; then will I hear from heaven, and will forgive their sin, and will heal their land. II Chronicles 7:14

Humble yourself and turn away from that sin that so easily entangles you!

Father, we thank you that we join our faith together to enter boldly into your presence. We thank you for the blood of Jesus that gives us access into your holy presence. You are worthy, and we bless and adore you Lord, God. You deserve all of the glory and honor for you alone are great and mighty.

Thank you, Lord, for your goodness towards us, and we ask that you forgive us for all of our iniquities. You said that if we would confess our sins, that you would be faithful and just to forgive us and to cleanse us from all unrighteousness. Lead us today in the path of righteousness for your namesake. Order our steps in your word. Lead us and guide us into the things that you would have us to do today so that we will give you glory. Bless us to be at the right place at the right time.

Thank you for the blood that covers our homes and this country. Thank you for keeping us safe from terrorism. Thank you for keeping our children and our grandchildren safe while we are absent one from another. Thank you for the angels that you have given charge over our lives that are walking with us and protecting us. Thank you for this abundant life that you have given to us. Thank you for being a shield all around us, and we hold up the shield of faith against the attacks of the enemy. We shall not be moved from our position of faith, and we thank you that you are a rewarder to those who diligently stand in position.

Thank you for anointing us to represent you. Thank you that we have the authority and the power to overcome evil with good, and we declare today that we are going to walk in the good. We will walk in an excellent spirit and not a wrong spirit.

Demolish the enemy with your strong arm and scatter them out of our way. Remind us that we have the power of love and a sound mind for we are anointed and appointed. We are the head and not the tail. We are your children called by your name. Bless us to rise and walk in authority and power.

Thank you for uncommon favor with you and with man. We declare that we will walk in an excellent spirit. We will yield to the Holy Spirit, and we will obey your word. We will be the light in this dark world, and we pray for the salvation of those who are held captive by the enemy. We pray that they are set free right now by the power of your Holy Spirit.

Release more of your love in us that we may represent you on earth. Expand our territory and give us an opportunity to be an influence for your namesake. We love you, Lord. In Jesus name. Amen

DAY 13

I beseech you therefore, brethren, by the mercies of God, that ye present your bodies a living sacrifice, holy, acceptable unto God, which is your reasonable service. Romans 12:1

Yield your will to God's will.

We thank you for another day in which you have allowed us to open our eyes and witness your goodness on earth. We thank you for the access that the blood of Jesus has given us into your presence, and we are honored that we can come boldly to receive from you.

Thank you for loving us so much. We honor and glorify you, and we lift you up for you alone are holy. You are mighty, and there is no other God but you. Thank you for delivering us out of darkness into your marvelous light.

Lord, we pray that you would forgive us for all of

our iniquities and all of our sins; those things that have been woven into our character and personality that cause us to do wrong when we want to do right. We pray that the blood of Jesus would cleanse us from all unrighteousness. Create in us a clean heart that we may be acceptable in your presence.

Lord, we thank you for blessing us with another day of favor. Thank you for blessing this country and for watching over our children and our grandbabies. Thank you so much for your kindness towards us and the benefits that we have in you.

Thank you that we have power in your name by the blood of Jesus that covers, empowers and protects us. Thank you that our feet are on the head of our enemies because greater are you on the inside of us than anything in the world.

Guard our tongue so that we will speak life and not curses. Bless us to be your peacemakers here on earth. Bless us to refrain from always trying to defend ourselves. We surrender our hearts to you and resist all unruly and self-centered attitudes. Reveal our true selves to us and bless us not to have a false identity. Reveal the wrong that is in our lives because we want to be better. Holy Spirit teach us how to walk and how to love you.

We make a decision to release unforgiveness that has held us in bondage. We release those weights off of us right now in the name of Jesus. We refuse to continue being victims living in the bondage of unforgiveness. Refresh and renew our spirits and our souls. Thank you for setting us free to enjoy all of the promises that you have released in our lives, Lord.

We command the spirit of confusion and disorder to get out of our lives, in Jesus name. We refuse to continue to procrastinate; we are going to do what you have commanded us to do. Help us to know your voice and to live with an excellent spirit. Thank you that you haven't given us a spirit of fear but of power, love, and a sound mind. We are a fearless people; we are your children, and we have authority, dominion, and power here on earth. Teach us how to walk it out today.

We declare a supernatural increase in all areas of our lives. Give us your wisdom to manage the resources that you release and remind us to give so that it may be used to bless others when we receive it. Enlarge our capacity to love and teach us how to love those outside of our circle of friends and family.

We trust you, Lord, and we will not waver. Our mind is made up, and our feet are planted on the solid rock. We are unmovable abounding in your word. Knowing that our labor is not in vain and that what we do for you is going to last forever.

We love you, and we thank you for the angels that you have given charge over our lives. We thank you that we can have this relationship with you and that we can talk with you, and we know that you hear us. Thank you for answered prayer. We give you glory, and we celebrate you. In Jesus name. Amen

DAY 14

Let us come before his presence with thanksgiving, and make a joyful noise unto him with psalms. Psalm 95:2

Take a moment to thank God for everything that comes into your mind.

Father, we love you, and we praise you. We thank you for allowing us to open our eyes this morning to have another experience in your presence. Lord, we enter into your presence with humility and we ask that you would forgive us for all of our sins. We are so thankful that you love us in spite of ourselves and in spite of our shortcomings. Your love is truly amazing.

We thank you that we have oneness with you, and we thank you that we have life with you now and forever. Lord, you are holy, and you are worthy of all praise, and we ask that you bless us to walk holy, putting nothing before you, not our children, not our marriages, nothing.

We thank you for protecting us from chaos, terrorism and from anything that could cause us harm. We thank you for protecting this country, and we thank you for protecting our children and loved ones. We thank you for being faithful in our lives and being a covering over us.

We pray that we would love and live, today, in a way that would show others that you are a loving God. Let your righteousness, peace, and joy be our signet today that people may have hope. We pray that you break off any negative word that has been spoken over our lives or the lives of our children, families, and members of your body. We pray that every curse spoken will be broken. Send the laborers to our children and our grandchildren that they may get in line with your perfect will.

We pray that your Kingdom will come, and your will be done on earth as it is in heaven. Put to shame those who wish evil upon us. Give us a fresh touch today, Lord. Overtake us and the people of God, as we sit in your presence and praise you together. We pray that our praise and worship will be a symphony to you.

Oh, God, we proclaim your goodness today, and we proclaim salvation and deliverance will go forth today. We pray right now in the name of Jesus that you will bless us to exercise our right to speak your word, and we declare favor in the name of Jesus. We call forth supernatural increase. We declare today in the name of Jesus that our homes are blessed, that our finances are blessed, that our health is blessed and that we walk in the promises that you gave to Abraham.

We thank you that we can speak a thing and it shall come to pass. Bless us to walk in integrity and not walk as those that have no hope. We walk in your power and your will. Lord, order our steps today that we may move according to your direction.

Bless us to extend your love to all those that we encounter today. Give us discernment that we may give whatever is needed in due season to help others. Guide us skillfully, Lord, by your hand. Bring conviction when our motives are wrong and keep a muzzle on our tongue. Lord, bless us to be people who will not gossip and judge or condemn, but bless us to speak life.

Oh, God, we declare a day of releasing of provision for our lives. Do the supernatural as only you can. We love you and we salute you. We are honored to be called by your name, and we are blessed to be your children. In Jesus name. Amen.

DAY 15

Be careful for nothing; but in every thing by prayer and supplication with thanksgiving let your requests be made known unto God.   Phil. 4:6

Don't worry, God has got it! Be thankful and bless His name.

Father, we thank you for being such a good God for you alone are worthy. You deserve all the glory, and all the honor and we celebrate you. We magnify you together, Lord. God, you are incredible, and your mercy endures to all generations. We thank you for your grace and your mercy.

Father, we come in the name of Jesus asking that you will forgive us for all of our sins and from anything that is hidden that only you know. Wash us clean by the blood of Jesus and create in us a clean heart and renew a right spirit within us. We repent and we receive your forgiveness in the name of Jesus.

Thank you for your faithfulness towards us. Thank you, Father, that when we fall we can get back up in your love, because of your covenant promise. Thank you for every provision that you have released into our lives and for the protection that you have given to us. Give us revelation to know clearly your will and your way. Order our steps that you may be glorified and that we may be at the right place at the right time.

Bless us to be a blessing to others that you may get the glory here on earth. Bless us to guard our hearts and not to allow our hearts to receive a negative and doubtful word. Bless us to speak your word over our lives consistently and diligently. For your word shall surely come to pass in our lives. Maximize our faith to believe the impossible and bless us to know that all things are possible to those that believe. Bless us not to be doubtful people but bless us to be able to wait for that time of manifestation. Bless us to hold onto our faith during the process.

Bless us to yield our will to yours that you may speak to us and guide us into your promises. Bless us to overcome evil with good so that when evil tries to overtake us we will operate in the kindness of your love; for love covers a multitude of sins. God, bless us to represent you with an excellent spirit. Bring conviction if we operate in a rude spirit, bring conviction that will change us. Bless us to repent and turn from our wicked ways and bless your presence to consume us from the inside out. We want more of you.

Bless us to know that you have given us the authority to conquer and take dominion. Bless us to begin to rise and possess with boldness. Give us spiritual eyes that we can see people beyond their smiles. Give us discernment that we can see their condition and know what's happening in our environment so that we can pray for those concerns. Bless us not to talk about it but to be about it.

Bless us to be humble people that we may receive the blessings that we have prayed for and that when we are broken, you will heal and restore us.

Lord, bless us not to be sensitive and vulnerable, knowing that it takes time for you to heal and restore. Where we are confused, give us clarity. Where we are disturbed, release peace.

Bless us to listen to you as you give us instructions and bless us not to talk ourselves out of our blessings, but to listen and obey. Remind us that we are children of the most high God; a royal priesthood, clothed in righteousness.

Release supernatural opportunities that we never even dreamed about. We declare open doors today, and we bind up every demonic spirit that is trying to keep the door closed that you have ordained to stay open. We join our faith together right now in the name of Jesus, and we declare open doors over our lives and our families.

We pray right now for debt cancellation and that you would give us the discipline to pay the debts and use money according to your purpose. Bless our minds and bodies to be healed today. God bless us to represent your goodness on earth for you are good.

Use us for the up building of your Kingdom. We love you and give you glory and honor for you alone are worthy of all the praise. Thank you for being our God. In Jesus name. Amen.

DAY 16

And when ye stand praying, forgive, if ye have ought against any: that your Father also which is in heaven may forgive you your trespasses. Mark 11:25

Forgive others and forgive yourself.

Father, we thank you for access into your presence. We thank you for the covenant that we have with you by the blood of Jesus, that we are one with you. You are good, and your mercy endures to all generations; mercies which are new every morning. We thank you for the grace that you have released into our lives, and we don't take this for granted. We know that we have been purchased with the blood of Jesus and that we are your children.

Thank you for being the source of our supply and for being faithful and true to your word. Thank you for being a God of integrity. Teach us how to live in your strength. Teach us how to live in your power.

Teach us how to manifest your ability in our lives and teach us how to walk boldly in faith.

Bless us not to be hindered by fear, but bless us to keep advancing in the things of you. Teach us how to operate in your glory. Bless us with spiritual ears that we may hear you even now.

Remove all that stuff that has cluttered our hearts. Give us a tender heart, a heart of mercy and grace. Bless our passion to be elevated. Bless us to fall in love with you and to be single-mindedly focused on you. Remove the yoke of oppression off of our lives and the yoke from our thoughts. All former things have passed away, behold all things have become new.

Father, loose confusion against any Satanic and demonic spirits that are coming against our lives. Bless us not to live a slothful life but to be consistent in our relationship with you. Bless us not to be so caught up in the world that we fail to read your word and to talk with you and worship you. Bless us to run in the way of your commandments and not in the way that we want to go, but in the way that you would have us to.

We receive the plans that you have for us, plans for good and not evil and we thank you that this is our set time, and we don't want to miss this moment of favor. Bless us to walk in your anointing for this is the day that you have made, and we will be glad and rejoice in it. We will not walk in this day depressed and confused, but we will walk in this day with expectation and unspeakable joy because of your goodness.

Increase and prosper our way and bless us to be a blessing and influence in your kingdom. Bless us to show your love everywhere we go and to walk in your grace and humility so that you will get all the glory. In Jesus name. Amen

DAY 17

The Lord will give strength unto his people; the Lord will bless his people with peace. Psalm 29:11

Pray to God; He will give you peace.

Father, God, we thank you for your divine favor over our lives, and we give thanks to you for you are good. You are great, and you are sovereign, and we thank you for all that you have done for us.

Lord, you have prepared your throne in the heavens and your Kingdom rules over all. We thank you for the blood of Jesus that secured our salvation, and we thank you that we can come boldly into your presence asking for forgiveness of sins.

We thank you for your word being true and that you do all that you said you would do. We thank you for the provision that you have released into our homes for food on our tables and clothing on our backs. Bless our faith not to fail that we may fulfill the mandate that you have ordained to take place in our lives today.

Touch all of our hearts right now in the name of Jesus and release more of your glory. Bless us to know that we are a prosperous people and that we are strong and mighty in you. Bless us to walk in understanding. Bless us to overcome evil with good. Bless us to walk in an excellent spirit. Bless us to walk in integrity. Bless us not to be mean, rude, crude and judgmental but bless us to walk as you would have us to walk. Bless our latter to be greater than our former.

Release your glorious presence and overtake us. Let your glory be revealed in our lives, Lord, and give us a spirit of wisdom and revelation. Open the eyes of our understanding that we may know the mystery of your will. Increase our knowledge, wisdom, peace, love, joy and prosperity.

Bless us not to be self-consumed and bring a Holy Ghost conviction when we step out of your will to let us know. Set us free today. Let your word increase in our lives that our faith may also increase.

Bless our children to rise and walk in your word. Thank you that we are joint heirs with Christ Jesus and that we have the victory in you. Increase our faith that we may obtain every spiritual blessing that you have released into our lives. Bless us to be doers of the word and not hearers only. Bless us to walk in an active faith that moves on what we believe.

Thank you for supplying all of our needs in Christ Jesus. Thank you for commanded blessings. Keep us protected from the enemy and bless our conversations so that we just won't say anything. Bless us to know that we are held captive by the words that we speak, so bless our words to be positive and of a good report.

Bless our motives to be sincere and Lord, we pray, that your will be done in our lives. You are excellent, oh, God. In Jesus name. Amen

DAY 18

Casting all your care upon him; for he careth for you. I Peter 5:7.

Give God all of your cares.

Lord, God, we magnify your greatness for you are good and greatly to be praised. We glorify you, and our souls magnify you. God, you are wonderful, and there is no other like you. Thank you for this new day that you have made, and we will rejoice and be glad in it.

Father, we ask right now, in the name of Jesus, that you would forgive us for all of our sins and all of our iniquities and that you would cleanse us from the inside out. Make us righteous in your sight and lead us in the path of righteousness for your namesake. Lord, we thank you for your mercies that are new each and every morning.

Thank you for the opportunity to be used by you

and bless us to walk as vessels of honor and integrity. We thank you for being a God of integrity and for remaining faithful to your word. We thank you for your beautiful word of truth and how excellent is your name in all the earth.

Lead us in the steps that you have marked out for us this day. Lead and guide us into the plans that you have for us which we know are good and not evil, for a future and a hope. Give us ears to hear what you are saying to us, Lord, and give us an obedient spirit to yield to your will.

Bless us to chase after you and teach us how to guard our hearts and our emotions so that we will not be manipulated by the enemy. Bless us not to be held captive by the enemy, but teach us how to be honest with ourselves and not live in deception, fooling ourselves and lacking the maturity that we need to have in you. Bless us to be reminded of the man in the mirror and to work out our own salvation. Bless us to be more like you and to live like you.

Lord, break down every stronghold that has

controlled our nature and our personalities. We want to be effective in your kingdom. Bless us to represent you here on earth so that people will see your goodness. Bless us with the spirit of unity and oneness. Allow us to link our arms and hearts together and edify one another, not tearing each other down, but always seeing the good. Let us be a people who will always show that you are God of love.

Teach us how to love unconditionally, even when it hurts. Teach us how to forgive quickly and to edify others more highly than ourselves. Bless us not to be people caught up in self-righteousness. Remove pride from our spirit and our hearts. Teach us not to be so easily offended, not to be so easily hurt. Give us a spiritual nature that we can take a licking and keep on ticking. Let us keep loving, keep serving and keep worshiping you with a sincere heart.

Teach us how to strive in adversity; how to abide through trials and challenges that will come our way. Teach us how to allow your Holy Spirit to transform us from the inside out. Make us uncomfortable that we may be more like you. Get us out of our safe zone and teach us how to begin to walk by faith. Teach us how to grow and how to have joy regardless of what is happening in our lives. The joy of the Lord is our strength, and we find joy in you. Thank you for strengthening us when are weak.

We're excited that our eyes haven't seen, our ears haven't heard nor has it entered into our hearts the things that you have made ready for us; the things that you have prepared for our marriages, our children, our grandchildren, our churches, our finances and our future. We're excited about the favor that you have given us, and we are going to pursue you with all of our hearts; that in everything, you will get the glory.

We love you, Lord, we bless your name, and we thank you for this day. In Jesus name. Amen.

DAY 19

One thing have I desired of the Lord, that will I seek after; that I may dwell in the house of the Lord all the days of my life, to behold the beauty of the Lord, and to enquire in his temple. Psalm 27:4

Remain in His presence.

Father, we bless you, and we thank you for being a Father that gives us access into your presence in the holy of holies. We praise your name this day for you are worthy, and you hold all power in your hand. We bless you with all of our heart.

Father, we ask that you would forgive us for all of our sins and iniquities. Remove the enemy's influence that entangles us and cleanse us from all unrighteousness. Lord, we want to look like you, walk like you, and we want to represent you as your ambassadors here on earth. Order our steps this day as we seek to do your will.

We thank you for your faithfulness and for your mercy which endures for all generations. Thank you for covering us through the night. Thank you for the blood of Jesus that covers our doorpost and thank you for protecting our children, our grandbabies, and this country. We don't take that for granted, Lord.

Thank you for our salvation and for being the supplier of all of our needs according to your riches in glory in Christ Jesus. Thank you for always being there; we can depend on you for you are faithful.

We thank you that our storehouses are blessed, our children are blessed, and we are a blessed people because of your presence on the inside of us. Lord, please make us to be tools of peace. Bless us, right now, in the name of Jesus, that instead of bitterness and resentment, we will be quick to forgive and not allow the devil to grip our emotions and take us out of position in your presence.

Teach us how to stand firmly grounded in your word and your love and righteousness. Bless us not to be manipulated out of self-righteousness and pride, but bless us to be humble and lowly of heart. Bless our faith not to fail in anything. Bless us to be content in you for you are our satisfaction, and we love you. There is no other like you, and we can't live without you.

Examine our hearts and if you find anything that is not of you, remove it, Lord. As we pursue perfection, bless us to put away childish things and teach us how to be strong in the word and let no evil attach itself to our minds. Put to shame those who wish evil on our lives and scatter our enemies today. Confuse our enemies and let no weapon formed against us prosper.

Bless us to be people that would give you glory. Open up heaven over our lives and give us more of you, more of your power. Bless us to have room enough to receive it. Bless us to be givers so that whenever we see a need we will be moved to give. Bless us to learn to give so that we can receive more. Bless us to learn to live in the kingdom so that there will not be holes in our bags. Bless us to walk in your anointing that we may accomplish the work that you have laid on our lives to do. Bless us to be the examples to follow that when people look at us they will see your goodness.

We rebuke every demonic spirit that has tried to cause us to live in a place of poverty and lack. Oh, God, we are a blessed people. We are blessed because you are the blessor. Give us wisdom, Lord. Guide us Holy Spirit and give us a conviction to obey what the spirit is telling us to do. Bless us with wisdom to manage communications with others. Bless us with wisdom on our jobs, in our homes and our churches. We don't want to make the wrong decisions because of the flesh.

Let us walk in our God-given authority with boldness to believe for miracles, signs, and wonders in a huge way. We want to experience your glory. Give us eyes to see your works. Speak to our hearts so that we will be strengthened by your wonderful word.

Command your blessings upon our lives, even right now. We pray for the salvation of our family members today. Send your angels, in the name of Jesus, to overtake every demonic force that is trying to hold them back. Save their souls, Father. Send your angels to protect our prayers so that they will prosper.

Thank you for the blessings that you have released into our lives today. Thank you for the power of the blood of Jesus that has enabled us to walk this walk. In Jesus name. Amen.

DAY 20

Pray without ceasing. I Thess. 5:17

Never stop praying!

Father, you are incredible, and you are an awesome wonder. Just your existence in our lives is amazing, and we are grateful that we have a God who is touchable and relational. We honor you for that, Father. There is no other like you, and you are worthy of all praise. You are strong and mighty, and there is no one more powerful than you. No one wiser or more knowledgeable and we worship you. We bow down and surrender all in your presence. We love you, and we thank you for striving with us.

We come, in the name of Jesus, asking that you will forgive us for all those things that so easily attach to our character and our minds. We claim, by the glory of your goodness, that you will burn off every work that has attached itself to our hearts. Create in us a clean heart and renew a right spirit within us.

Clean us up, God, and allow us to stand in right standing by your side.

Thank you for your son, Jesus. Thank you for the living sacrifice that gave us life. Thank you for the blood that gives us access to your power and your authority. Thank you for your Holy Spirit. Thank you, Lord, that all of your promises are yes and amen. Thank you that you are the supplier and that we have no lack. Thank you for the anointing that encourages us when we are weak. We thank you, Lord, God that you are our defense.

Give us ears to hear you and bless our wills to become your will. Bless us not to be self-consumed with our thoughts and caught up with our emotions. Give us understanding so that your knowledge and wisdom will come easy to us. We pray that our life pleases you and gives you great delight. We want you to look down at our hearts and be pleased that you created us. Let the fruit of our lips prove your wisdom is right.

Teach us how to obey and be submissive to

those in authority who have rule over our lives. Bless us to be men and women of integrity and bless us not to walk in pride, but to walk in humility. Bless us to edify and encourage others. Bless us to be vessels of honor that can be used to heal the sick and to prophesy to those that are dying. Let our hands be your hands. Remove the enemy and destroy them with your strong arm. Scatter them out of our way, Lord.

We pray that you will bless us going in and coming out. We are blessed in the city and blessed in the field. We are blessed to be above and not beneath. Bless us to know that in spite of our circumstances we are walking in high places. Regardless of what we are going through here on earth, we are seated with you in heavenly places.

Teach us how to activate your power in our lives. Teach us how to walk victoriously and confidently. Teach us how to keep our joy and our peace. Lord, bless us to be strengthened and encouraged during times of transformation. Let us be blessed with dominion and victory each and every day. Let the windows of heaven be opened over our lives.

Teach us how to love your words and stir up a passion that will cause us to love you, not for the things that you give us, but just because of who you are. We pray that you would stir up the passion, zeal, and boldness on the inside of us that we would be bold in your name. Bless us to stand and be a witness for your glory in this dark world. Bless us to be a people that are well pleasing to you.

Overtake every principality that is trying to hold up our blessings and prevent us from walking into a wealthy place. We claim victory right now in the name of Jesus. We are a prosperous people in you Lord, God. Release the mantle of power and authority in our lives. In Jesus name, Amen.

DAY 21

Therefore I say unto you, What things soever ye desire, when ye pray, believe that ye receive them, and ye shall have them. Mark 11:24

Believe!

We praise you, Lord, for you are good. We praise you for your strength, your power and your excellent ways. We praise you, and we celebrate you for you are a good God, and we are so honored to come into your presence. We thank you for the blood of Jesus that gives us access.

We love you, and we magnify your name for you are holy. Forgive us for our sins, Lord. We ask that you would cleanse us with the blood of Jesus and make us righteous in your sight. Create in us a clean heart and renew a right spirit within us. We thank you for your loving kindness, for it is amazing.

We thank you for the hedge of protection and for your spirit that is always with us, in us, and around us. We thank you for your divine protection that covered us all through the night. We thank you for your faithfulness in our lives, and we thank you for another day that we have not experienced before. We thank you for allowing us always to be on your mind.

Holy Spirit, take control of our day and be glorified. We surrender everything to you, and we recognize that every good thing that we have is from you, Lord, God. Shine your light on your word and direct our paths today. Make allowance for our feet so that we will not stumble. Bring conviction, in the name of Jesus. Illuminate your word in our hearts and shine in those dark places.

Lord, bless us to be able to carve out time to be alone with you to feed on your truth. Bless us to learn your word that we may know you. We want you to have total control over our lives. Bless us not to wander around in the wilderness of life. We take authority over our thoughts, and we bind all spheres of fantasy and oppression wherever we find them, and we cast them down in the name of Jesus.

We cancel all the plans of the enemy against our lives and our children's lives, and we declare every evil spirit cast out in the name of Jesus.

Teach us how to walk this walk that we may be mature and be all that you have called us to be. Teach us to be God consumed. Teach us how to move in love. Teach us how to love the unlovable. Teach us how to forgive and how to remove offense from our lives. Teach us how to bind up demons. Teach us how to lay hands on the sick and to speak a word in prophecy knowing that you are speaking to us. Bless us to decrease so that your Holy Spirit would increase. Let the power of your word and your work be evident in our lives. Display your awesome power that man would begin to believe.

Send your angels to prosper our way today and let them fight for us in the heavens against principalities and rulers of darkness. We claim a new season in the name of Jesus, and we claim a fresh anointing. Holy Spirit you are welcome in this place. Command your blessings upon our lives, every blessing with our name on it. Bless your angels to bring it to pass by the power of your Holy Spirit. We love you, and we give you all praise. In Jesus name. Amen.

STAY CONNECTED

<u>*Kim Lyons Ministries*</u>

Connect with Kim Lyons Ministries through these social media Channels:

Facebook.com/Kim Lyons

<u>*Twitter.com/@Kimlyons2012*</u>

Instagram/@Kimlyonsministries

Website:

www.kimlyonsministries.com

60031591R00048

Made in the USA
Charleston, SC
22 August 2016